GREY-GREEN
COACHES & BUSES

ANDREW MEAD

AMBERLEY

To my dear friends:
Tracy & Stephen and their children Alexander & Emily
For sharing so many happy times together!

First published 2016

Amberley Publishing
The Hill, Stroud
Gloucestershire, GL5 4EP

www.amberley-books.com

Copyright © Andrew Mead, 2016

The right of Andrew Mead to be identified as
the Author of this work has been asserted in
accordance with the Copyrights, Designs and
Patents Act 1988.

ISBN 978 1 4456 6376 0 (print)
ISBN 978 1 4456 6377 7 (ebook)

British Library Cataloguing in Publication Data.
A catalogue record for this book is available from
the British Library.

Origination by Amberley Publishing.
Printed in the UK.

Contents

Introduction

This book is not intended to be a history of Grey-Green or its associated and parent companies. Several books have been previously published that fully detail the company's history. It is intended to complement the other books, and to be a nostalgic and historic photographic record of the vehicles and services operated mainly during the last fifty years of the company's operations, although the run up to this period is also illustrated.

Since a young age I have been interested in road transport, particularly motor coaches. It was one of the interests I inherited from my late father, Bill (known as W. J. Mead in photograph credits featured in other transport publications such as Ian Allan's *A History of the Devon General Omnibus and Touring Company Limited*). Maybe the interest originates from my father's ancestors: Charles Mead and his cousin Joseph (Joe) Walter Lodge (my second cousin twice removed). They started a bus service in around October 1920 between High Easter and Chelmsford in Essex. In November 1949, a former Orange Luxury Coaches Bedford WTB/Duple DXM 832 was acquired, with DXM 837 following in May 1950, both having been new in March 1937. The bus service eventually grew to become J. W. Lodge & Sons Ltd, and they trade now as 'Lodge Coaches of High Easter'. Joe, the younger brother of Robert, was born in Tooley Street, Bermondsey, London, SE1 on 14 April 1896 (a historic part of London and at one time a ship-building area). Meanwhile, just a few miles away across the River Thames, Charles George Ewer was establishing his business, which was later to become Grey-Green Coaches. Joe's father William Lodge and mother Lucy Mead had married in June 1893 in Lewisham, London, SE13. William had previously been a Metropolitan Police officer who had served W Division in south London for a short while. After William's sudden death in 1899, Joe's mother returned to her home village of High Easter with her two sons. Joe passed away on 6 August 1960 and the rest is history…

Living just outside the Grey-Green catchment area, I was brought up during the 1960s and 1970s with regular coach tours provided by Valliant-Cronshaw and their successor, Venture Transport of Harrow. We also travelled with Horseshoe Coaches of Tottenham and its subsidiaries – Lee's Luxury Coaches of Barnet and Moden Super Coaches of Enfield. Now, the only local company is Enfieldian Tours of Enfield, who still provide the traditional type of coach tour. There was also the occasional school outing during the early 1970s by coach, mainly to central London, which I adored; they included visits to London Zoo to see 'Guy', the gorilla. Both Finchley Coaches and Brunt's of Hatfield (Brunt's were later taken over by Sampson's Coaches of Cheshunt) were generally used by the school.

Grey-Green Coaches was originally a fleet name within the George Ewer Group. In 1978 I joined the Ewer Group Enthusiasts' Club. The club had been an idea of Colin Druce, who had held a meeting with a small number of Grey-Green staff – Ken Bateman, John Harris and David Hustings, who were keen enthusiasts – and decided that that there was enough interest to launch the club in March 1966. After joining I quickly became friends with club officers Owen Woodliffe and the late Ken Bateman (who suddenly passed away at the young age of fifty-five in January 2001). I later became friends with Grey-Green employees John Card, Jeremy Buck and Colin Druce. The club was renamed the Grey-Green Enthusiasts' Club in 1981, the year after the Cowie Group purchased the George Ewer Group, and in 1986 I became the club secretary. The club was sadly wound up in June 2000 after the Grey-Green name disappeared in favour of the corporate Arriva branding.

Although at the time I was not employed in the coaching industry, one of my roles in employment required me, from mid-1983, to assist in regulating the afternoon Kent Commuter coach departures from Bressenden Place in Victoria, London, SW1. Maidstone & District Motor Services were responsible for regulating all of the seventy or so departures operated by the various coach companies, and so I often used to work closely with Maidstone & District inspector Allen Hollands. Within two years the number of departures between 16.00 and 18.00 had grown to around ninety – with a coach leaving around every ninety seconds. Victoria coach station took over the responsibility from fellow National Bus Company subsidiary Maidstone & District during the mid-1980s and, a few months later, Grey-Green and Reliance of Gravesend took on the role. I continued to assist their inspectors at Bressenden Place, so very occasionally worked with Grey-Green inspector George Green. Over a period of time I got to know many of the Kent-based Grey-Green drivers, who included Paul Cohen, Peter Darling, Steve Davis, Dave Filby, Steve Price and Paul Shepherd.

Owen Woodliffe (left) and Ken Bateman looking after the 'Grey-Green Enthusiasts' Club' sales stand at the Strood depot open day on 2 December 1990. Ken and Owen have written several books about the George Ewer Group, both together and individually.

During October 1991, around half a mile away from Bressenden Place, the Green Line coach station opened at Bulleid Way (named after the Southern Railway engineer Oliver Bulleid). At the same time, Golden Tours Ltd and Green Line Coaches opened offices at No. 4/4a Fountain Square, adjacent to Bulleid Way. I was very fortunate to assist Luton & District Green Line staff Clive King and Roger Blunden in the coach station in my same role and, in 2000, Geoff Walker replaced Roger, all three being transport enthusiasts. My job role changed in late 2003 and so visits to the coach station ceased. Little did I know that in the summer of 2016, some twenty-five years after it opened, I'd be working there in the coaching industry after a change of employer and job, back with Geoff again enjoying a chat over a coffee – but that's another story!

Most of the photographs in this book have been taken by me, while others have come from a variety of sources, including being inherited or purchased from many transport events. I thank everyone who have supplied photographs from their collections, including Paul Bateson, Jim Blake, John Harris, my old boss Syd Tombleson, Tony Wilson and Owen Woodliffe. Where known I have credited the original photographer and/or the origin of the photograph. I have tried to make the photograph captions as informative and interesting as possible and, where applicable, the Ewer or Cowie vehicle fleet number is always shown first.

Grateful thanks must go to former Grey-Green staff John Card and the late Ken Bateman, while further thanks are due to other former Grey-Green staff including Paul Bateson, John Harris, Richard Howden, Paul Shepherd, John Wilks, as well as Owen Woodliffe who was casual staff. Other thanks go to Sheila Henthorne, Andrew Lodge, and Tony Zotti MBE. Special thanks must go to my good friend Stephen May for all his hard work scanning photographs and other help.

Andrew Mead
Barnet, Greater London
May 2016

The author stands next to former Grey-Green 887 (E887 KYW), which carries the last Maidstone & District livery before the corporate Arriva livery was introduced. 887 passed to Maidstone & District via London Coaches (Kent) during May 1996. It is now in preservation and owned by Daniel Hardcastle. It is seen at the Cobham Bus Museum Spring Gathering at Brooklands on 17 April 2016. (Rosa Reale)

I

The Origins of the 'George Ewer Group'

The Years to the Second World War

The origins of Grey-Green can be traced back to 1885 when Charles George Ewer commenced the hiring of handcarts to traders in Shoreditch, east London. In 1892 he had acquired a former greengrocer's shop at No. 78 Leonard Street in Shoreditch from which to run his now established business. By 1900 the business had expanded into the operation of horses and carriages for the transportation of coal, furniture and other general goods. Stables were situated in Bateman's Row underneath the North London Railway viaduct. Charles George Ewer died in 1910 and the business, which now comprised of three horse-drawn carts, passed to his eldest son, the fourteen-year-old James Henry Ewer. It was discovered in 1915 that another unrelated Charles Ewer was trading as a carman nearby. So it was decided that the name 'Charles George Ewer' be shortened to 'George Ewer'. After the First World War, motor vehicles were introduced to deliver goods and at weekends a lorry fitted with old cinema seats was used to convey passengers on day trips. Charabanc excursions to the coast commenced in the early 1920s and the 'Grey-Green' name was now in use.

In 1930 a detached Victorian house with a large rear garden was acquired at No. 55 Stamford Hill, London, N16. The house was converted into offices, while a large, purpose-built garage to accommodate the coach fleet (which stood at approximately forty coaches) was built on the rear land. The area to the front of the house was converted to a hard standing area. The former house became the registered office of George Ewer Group the following year. The semi-detached house and garden next door, No. 53, were acquired in 1950 and converted into offices, while a purpose-built workshop was constructed in the rear garden for the Group.

During the following years various small operators were acquired. The first was Eva's Motor Coaches of Shoreditch during 1934, which was a reformed company of Joseph Eva and Albert Ewer's Royal Blue Coaches. Albert Ewer was a younger brother of James Henry Ewer, who had been operating in fierce competition with his brother for several years. Sid Page of Gorleston was also acquired the same year, which added licences to operate to Great Yarmouth.

A posed view
of Leylands and
Maudslays on the
forecourt of No. 55
Stamford Hill during
the summer, *c.* 1930.
Left to right: GJ 5910,
GJ 5912, GF 6673,
GJ 5911, GJ 3476 and
UW 8904. (Grey-Green
Coaches: Andrew
Mead Collection)

This 1931 Leyland,
GO 1042, leads a
line of vehicles in
Hyde Park in 1937,
transporting Indian
Army troops in
connection with
the Coronation.
(Grey-Green Coaches:
Andrew Mead
Collection)

An advertisement
dating from *c.* 1930,
showing Leyland
coaches of the time.
(Phil Moth Collection)

The War Years through to the Swinging Sixties

During the Second World War, many of Ewer's vehicles were requisitioned for military use and several important contracts were undertaken for the military.

Ardley Bros of Tottenham and Fallowfield & Britten of Hackney were acquired in 1952.

The well-respected and established operator Orange Luxury Coaches of Brixton, London, SW9 was purchased in October 1953. The firm had been established in 1920 as a trading name of Keith & Boyle (London) Ltd. The company was owned by partners Edward Keith Davies and Frank Boyle Monkman. In 1927 the large garage at Effra Road in Brixton was built. Shamrock & Rambler of No. 77 Holdenhurst Road, Bournemouth, was acquired in 1929 and adopted the Orange livery. Both operators named their coaches instead of allocating them fleet numbers. After Ewer acquired Keith & Boyle Ltd, it was renamed to Orange Luxury Coaches Ltd. Shamrock & Rambler went to Red & White and became a subsidiary of the National Bus Company in 1969. Orange had held the Royal Warrant for a number of years for transporting the royal household between Buckingham Palace and Sandringham House. Coaches therefore carried the royal coat of arms of the United Kingdom next to the Orange fleet name.

Over the years a few coach stations have been located in King's Cross and, during 1954, a purpose-built coach station in Pentonville Road, on the corner on Northdown Street, was opened. This coach station had replaced the nearby Judd Street coach station, which opened in 1947. The vehicle entrance was in Northdown Street – opposite the exit of what was to become the Eastern National coach station in 1963. The coach station was operated by PSV Operators Ltd and was served by various other operators, who included Norfolk Motor Services, Suttons of Clacton, Wallace Arnold and Yelloway. Colin Druce was an inspector there during weekends in the early 1960s, while Ken Bateman commenced working there in July 1965. The coach station closed at the end of October 1965, although its buildings had been demolished

Acquired with the business of Ardley Bros in 1952 was this Bedford OB, VME 109, seen in King's Cross coach station during the mid-1950s. (R. H. G. Simpson)

Orange MXV 77, a Bedford, was acquired with the company in 1953. It was named 'Eva' and passed to Fallowfield & Britten in 1959 before its disposal the following year. It is seen here at rest outside the Brixton garage during the 1950s. (Unknown: Andrew Mead Collection)

a few years previously. Services then picked up at road-side in Midland Road before Grey-Green and Yelloway relocated into the Britannia Airways terminal in Mabledon Place on 1 March 1966, while other services went to the new Caledonia Street coach station. Grey-Green moved its services again on 2 October 1967 to the nearby Eastern National coach station when the Essex Coast Pool commenced; however, the now-joint services commenced from Victoria coach station. The Eastern National coach station continued to be used until it closed in October 1976. Meanwhile, in 1968, Yelloway relocated to Caledonia Street and was used by Grey-Green as a pick-up point for their tours programme.

Grey-Green's first garage outside London was located at No. 33 Jackson Road in Clacton, sited opposite the Eastern National bus station. It opened in the mid-1930s and closed during 1960. After closure, the departure and arrival point moved to Wash Lane coach station. During the 1950s and 1960s Clacton was an extremely popular destination, whether for day trips or holidays. Many coaches could be found parked at various locations in this small Essex coastal town. Locally based operator Suttons was established in 1928 by George Sutton at No. 54 Pier Avenue. Before the Essex Coast Pool was formed, Grey-Green's Clacton-bound services had a fifteen-minute refreshment stop just outside Chelmsford at the early-nineteenth-century inn, the Widford White Horse Hotel in London Road, Widford. London-bound services stopped on the opposite side of the road, and passengers had to cross the dual carriageway to reach the inn. This refreshment stop was in use from at least 1948 until the end of the summer timetable in 1964. During the winter of 1964/5, there was no refreshment stop. Then, from summer 1965, the Duke of Wellington public house at nearby Hatfield Peveral was used, where Grey-Green joined fellow London operators such as Empires Best of Commerce Road, Wood Green, London, N22 (who were owned from July 1960 by Charles W. Banfield Ltd of Nunhead Lane, Peckham, London, SE15) and A. Timpson & Sons Ltd of No. 175 Rushey Green, Catford,

300 (SJJ 300) departs from the PSV Operators' King's Cross coach station in Pentonville Road during the late 1950s to early 1960s. 300 was new in March 1956 and sold in March 1964; it was the first coach to be numbered in the consecutive sequence. (Unknown: Andrew Mead Collection)

594 (YYX 594H), a Leyland, was captured leaving the Eastern National Omnibus Company coach station at Northdown Street in King's Cross while on route to Ipswich and Felixstowe during the early 1970s. The coach station was opened in May 1963 and was closed in October 1976. (Robert Mack: Andrew Mead Collection)

London, SE6 (Alexander Timpson had started his motor coach business in 1912 from premises at No. 22 Woodhurst Road, Plumstead, London, SE2). This halt remained in use until at least summer 1977. The Chelmsford stop for Grey-Green's Clacton service was at the railway station in Victoria Road before the services relocated into the Eastern National bus station when 'the pool' was formed. Another comfort stop used during the 1950s and early 1960s was also on the outskirts of Chelmsford; it was the eighteenth-century coaching inn, the White Hart in Colchester Road at Springfield. This location was, in general, used by excursion and private hire traffic.

Classique of Leyton became part of the Ewer Group in 1956. During the early 1960s, further small coach firms were acquired by Ewer's, which included: Batten Coaches of London, E6, in 1963; Viney's of London, N15, in 1964; and United Service Transport of London, SW, in October 1965.

582 (WLT 582G) lays over at Wash Lane coach station in Clacton, Essex, *c.* 1970. The Bedford was new in 1969 and sold in 1974, having passed to the Birch fleet in 1971. (Brian Botley)

MLK 952, a Leyland with a Harrington body, waits outside the 'Widford White Horse Hotel' while en route for Clacton during the 1950s. (Unknown: Andrew Mead Collection)

310 (SJJ 310), also a Leyland/Harrington, takes a break at the White Hart at Springfield during the late 1950s. (Phil Moth Collection)

611 (EMD 611J) waits in Chelmsford bus station shortly after delivery in the summer of 1971. Note the paper name displayed in the destination aperture. (Unknown: Andrew Mead Collection)

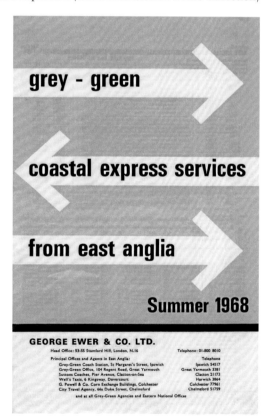

The front cover of the summer 1968 East Anglian Express services. (Andrew Mead Collection)

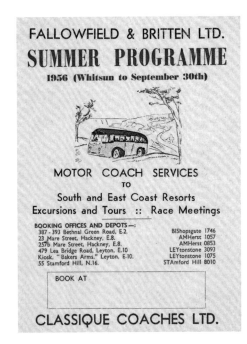
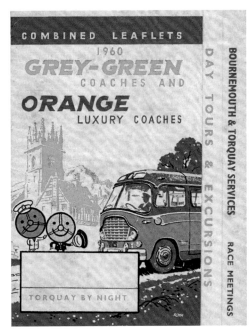

Above left: The front cover of the summer 1956 Fallowfield & Britten and Classique Coaches Ltd timetable. (Andrew Mead Collection)

Above right: The front cover of the 1960 Grey-Green and Orange tours and excursions leaflet. (Andrew Mead Collection)

During 1964, Grey-Green, with other Ewer companies, commenced operation of a rail replacement service for London Transport on the Northern Line between the Drayton Park and Finsbury Park Underground stations while construction work was carried out on the new Victoria Line. London Transport inspectors controlled the service and checked the tickets. A bus shelter was erected in Bryantwood Road at the side of Drayton Park station for passenger use. The peak vehicle requirement was for eighteen coaches, operating between 06.30 and 20.30; in contrast, on Sundays just four vehicles were required between 08.30 and 20.30. In general, the oldest coaches in the fleet were used. These included six coaches acquired from United Service Transport, which retained their livery and operated on the service until the last day, 31 August 1968, after which they were gradually sold.

During 1966 it was decided to phase out the Fallowfield & Britten, Battens, Viney, and Ardley names, leaving only those of Grey-Green and Orange in use.

As already stated, on 2 October 1967 Grey-Green commenced departures from the London Coastal Coaches-owned Victoria coach station, which had opened in 1932. They had entered into a pool with Eastern National Omnibus Company and Suttons of Clacton on the London Victoria–Clacton route. A few months later, Grey-Green joined forces with Eastern Counties Omnibus Company on the Great Yarmouth and Felixstowe routes. Grey-Green continued to depart from Victoria coach station on various services for the next thirty-one years.

382 (382 BLD) waits at the side of Drayton Park London Transport station in Bryantwood Road, London, N7, while operating on the Northern Line City Branch between Moorgate and Finsbury Park. A London Transport inspector (with his back to the camera) surveys the busy scene in *c.* 1965. (Phil Moth Collection)

This Bedford, 854 FXP, was acquired with United Services in October 1965. It was allocated to the Finsbury Park rail replacement service, and operated in United livery with Grey-Green names. (R. H. G. Simpson)

454 (ALR 4545B) was a Leyland/Harrington in the Battens fleet, seen in the late 1960s. (Wilf Rowley: Andrew Mead Collection)

Suttons of Clacton was a member of the Essex Pool. Their FOO 940, a Ford Thames with a Duple body, was new in 1962. It was sold in 1971. It is seen in Elizabeth Street outside Victoria coach station, having completed a service from Clacton *c.* 1970. Note the Westminster City Council road sweeper in the uniform cap looking at the camera. By him is a 'home-made' Metropolitan Police 'no waiting' sign; this type of sign remained in use until the mid-1980s. (Phil Moth)

715 (RYL 715R) leaves from the Elizabeth Street exit of Victoria coach station, *c.* 1977, after dropping its passengers. The 1930s-style lettering was removed after control of the building passed from the National Bus Company to London Regional Transport. (Phil Moth)

714 (RYL 714R), in 'Silver Jubilee' livery, is seen on Eccleston Bridge while en route to Victoria coach station, *c.* 1977–79. Visible behind the coach are some of the well-known old London Transport Green Line coach shelters, which lasted until mid-1991. To the rear is the warehouse of Bishop & Sons Removals. Joseph Bishop started his carriage and removal business in 1854, after leaving the Metropolitan Police, from premises in Elizabeth Street, where Victoria coach station would be built seventy-eight years later. The business later moved to this Hugh Street site and has since been redeveloped. (Unknown: Andrew Mead Collection)

East Staffordshire Council loaned this bus to Grey-Green during a rail strike in July 1982. 221 BTP is seen in Buckingham Palace Road when about to enter Victoria coach station for a service on the East Anglian Express. (Jim Blake)

Bedford 562 (NMU 562E) is seen inside the Southdown Motor Services coach station at Hilsea in Portsmouth in 1971 after a rear-end shunt. (Brian Bottley)

A 1951 Leyland, MLA 195, is seen on the forecourt of No. 55 Stamford Hill during the early 1950s. (Grey-Green Coaches: Andrew Mead Collection)

JLH 238, a 1948 Leyland, rests in the Fishmarket coach park at Hastings, probably in the early 1950s. The miniature railway track and the cliff lift are visible. (Unknown: Andrew Mead Collection)

In this early 1960s view, 379 (379 BLD) makes it way along Marine Drive in Margate, en route to the nearby town of Ramsgate. The 80-foot-high tower of the Dreamland cinema rises above the centre of the coach. The cinema opened in March 1935 and closed in November 2007. Its John Compton organ was last played in October 2004, and still remains in place. During the 1950s to the 1960s, the Dreamland coach park could accommodate around 100 coaches and many of their passengers can be seen on the sands. (Phil Moth collection)

This unregistered Harrington Crusader Mark II body is fitted on a Bedford SB8 chassis. It is from the batch 377–383 (377–383 BLD), which were new in November 1960. (Thomas Harrington Ltd of Hove: John Harris Collection)

Former Duple demonstrator Bedford VAL CLK 700B is seen at the 'Spring Tavern' at Wrotham in Kent while on an Orange tour to 'Historic Kent' on 20 March 1966. It carried a blue livery until October 1967. (John Harris Collection)

Fallowfield & Britten 396 (396 BLK) shows itself off at the seventh British Coach Rally in Brighton on 23 April 1961. Its sister coach, Orange 397 (397 BLK), was also entered into the rally. Both were new the previous month. (Bill Mead: Andrew Mead Collection)

445 (445 GYR) leaves the famous Black & White Motorways coach station in St Margaret's Road in Cheltenham (where passengers could change for connecting services), bound for Ipswich on the Estlander service during the late 1960s. From winter 1981 Richard Howden and Les Palmer were regular drivers on this service, which commenced in 1966. (Unknown: Andrew Mead Collection)

447 (447 GYR) rests in Edward Street coach park in Brighton during the late 1960s. Note The Black Lion pub to the right of the coach. (Phil Moth)

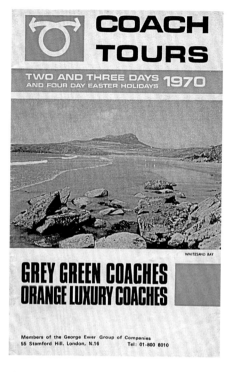

The front cover of the Easter 1970 tours brochure for Grey-Green and Orange. (Andrew Mead Collection)

Grey-Green had a club for regular coach travellers. This 1976 'Grey-Green Regular Travellers Club' membership card was issued to a late friend of the author – Ben Jenkins. Ben, who at the time lived in Muswell Hill, London, N10, was a founder member of the Post Office Vehicle Club and later formed 'Ride the Royal Mail Post Bus' for enthusiasts of post buses. (Ben Jenkins: Andrew Mead Collection)

The Last Decade of Ewer Ownership

On 1 January 1971, another well-known operator was acquired by the George Ewer Group. Birch Bros Transport Ltd of Royal Mail Yard, Cathcart Street, Kentish Town, London, NW5, which was formed in November 1899, decided to sell the remainder of the business. They had previously disposed of their final two-stage carriage services, routes 203 and 203M, between King's Cross and Rushden on 14 September 1969 to United Counties with twelve coaches. Ewer purchased the business with the remaining eleven Bedford and Seddon coaches, all of which were sold by November 1974. The Birch name continued to be used until October 1977. The Birch livery was white with a dark-red skirt. This livery style was then adopted for the rest of the Group's fleet. Grey-Green were given a green skirt and Orange Luxury were given an orange skirt.

In April 1974, 70 per cent of World Wide Coaches was purchased, while American Express owned the remaining 30 per cent. The yard at Nos 145–7 Coldharbour Lane, Brixton, London, SW9, was acquired with the company. A revised livery of white with a blue skirt was introduced to the fleet. World Wide Coaches Ltd was formed ten years before in April 1964. At the time of the takeover, they were the largest coach operator of Mercedes marque in the country. The remaining 30 per cent was acquired in January 1976. The Coldharbour Lane premises were sold in March 1978, and operations were moved to Plough Lane, Wimbledon, London, SW19.

Birch Bros VLF 37G, a Bedford, is seen at Gloucester Green, Oxford, captured by Oxford-based photographer R. H. G. Simpson. It was taken into the Ewer fleet on takeover in January 1971. (Andrew Mead Collection)

582 (WLT 582G), a Bedford, was transferred into the Birch fleet from Grey-Green in December 1971. (R. H. G. Simpson: Andrew Mead Collection)

703 (OYV 703R) was on a private hire job when seen at rest at Vere Road coach park in Broadstairs, Kent, on 25 May 1980. Housing has recently been built on this site. (Bill Mead: Andrew Mead Collection)

Gleaming Leyland 773 (YYL 773T) in World Wide colours is seen on 28 May 1980 leaving the St Stephen's Road, Canterbury, garage of East Kent Road Car Co. Ltd, after passing through the bus wash. The building of the garage was started just after the Second World War ended, but wasn't completed until 1948 due to the lack of materials. East Kent's Coach Works was located at the rear of the garage. (Andrew Mead)

777 (YYL 777T) was allocated to the World Wide fleet. World Wide won the contract from the Japan Travel Bureau to carry Japanese visitors in London. Bedford 777 is seen parked on the forecourt of No. 55 Stamford Hill on 21 April 1984, carrying contract livery for Japan Travel Bureau. The contract later passed to Horseshoe Coaches, and so the World Wide name was gradually dropped. (Paul Bateson)

Jack Wordsworth, the owner of Dix Luxury Coaches Ltd of Dagenham in Essex, retired on 2 February 1976 at the age of seventy and sold his business to the George Ewer Group. Jack formed his coach company in 1935. He wanted a catchy name for his new business and so adopted the 'Dix' name, which had originally been used on several restaurants owned by his brother Richard. Jack's first coach was an ex-London General AEC Regal. The fleet had grown to four by 1939 and to thirteen during the 1950s, consisting of various makes. From 1961 all purchases were of the local Ford marque. Dix held contracts with the Ford Motor Company of Dagenham to transport their workers to and from work. During June 1962 an hourly Sunday-only bus service was operated between Becontree Heath and Marks Gate Cemetery. The George Ewer Group acquired on takeover eleven coaches and one minibus. The Dix Travel agency was also acquired, being put under the control of Grey-Green Travel Ltd, while the Heath Garage yard in Wood Lane, Dagenham, continued to be rented.

The following month Universal Cream of Edmonton entered the George Ewer Group.

In December 1975, Orange Luxury Coaches Ltd was wound up, as the company had been making losses for some time and so the Brixton depot closed as an operational base on 7 December. However, the name continued to be used for a few more years, until the Royal Warrant expired. The following year on 1 March the former Classique coach station in Lea Bridge Road, Leyton, closed and was offered for sale. This just left the following operational coach depots in the Ewer Group: Brixton (World Wide), Edmonton, Dagenham (Dix), Mile End and Stamford Hill.

One of Jack Wordsworth's 'Dix' Ford / Duple coaches, MYY 992D, seen in the 1960s. (R. H. G. Simpson)

Dix FLA 998J was acquired with the company in February 1976. It is seen here on hire to Grey-Green during 1977 with 'Silver Jubilee' flags displayed each side of the vehicle registration number. (Unknown: Andrew Mead Collection)

Dix Ford/Plaxton 736 (SYU 736S) rests outside their yard in Wood Lane, Dagenham, on 25 July 1979. (Andrew Mead)

Dix 738 (SYU 738S) is seen here taking part in the twenty-fourth British Coach Rally at Brighton in April 1978. It had just been delivered to Dix and was a Ford R1114 with a Duple body. (Phil Moth)

Dix 800 (CYH 800V) had its Ford chassis shortened by Tricentral. It was part of a large private-hire job when seen on 5 June 1982 in Zion Place coach park in Margate. Just a few yards away was the office of local operator Blue Rambler Motor Coaches. (Bill Mead: Andrew Mead Collection)

613 (HMG 613K) was the only Mercedes operated by Grey-Green. It entered the fleet in August 1971 on demonstration and was bought in 1972. It was transferred to World Wide in November 1975. (Brian Botley)

Orange 398 (398 DLD) waits in Horse Guards Avenue, London, SW1, a once popular coach parking area at weekends that came to an abrupt end after the Downing Street bomb attack on 7 February 1991. To the rear of the coach is the main entrance of the Ministry of Defence building, while to the front is the Banqueting Hall – where Charles 1 was executed in 1649. The Bedford is seen during the early to mid-1960s. (Unknown: Andrew Mead Collection)

Orange 587 (WLT 587G) turns from Buckingham Palace Road into Semley Place before entering Victoria coach station in this early 1970s view. The tower block to the rear left is Portland House in Bressenden Place, while the roof over Victoria station platforms has been replaced by the Green Line coach station. The BOAC terminal is to the right. (Unknown: Andrew Mead Collection)

612 (GGH 612J) leaves Brighton by the way of Old Steine during the mid-1970s. It passed to Orange in January 1976 from Grey-Green and was sold in May 1978. Just visible to the rear is St Peter's Church, which was completed during 1828. (Gerard Walker: Andrew Mead Collection)

707 (TYE 707S), parked next to a Lacey's of East Ham, waits in the Cannon Road coach station at Ramsgate, just before departure on National Express service 001 to Victoria coach station via Catford and Brixton, on 3 June 1978. Note the black-on-yellow National route number label in the windscreen. Orange had one duty on this service during the summer of 1978. The regular driver on this service was Jack Cordwell. (Bill Mead: Andrew Mead Collection)

In 1979 just three coach subsidiaries were still trading – Dix, Grey-Green and World Wide, with a combined fleet of 125 vehicles. The George Ewer Group as the holding company also owned other subsidiary companies, which included motor dealers Burrell's of Ipswich and Bury St Edmunds, Page & Scott of Colchester, and Oakley's of Petersfield. Grey-Green Travel Limited ran a small number of local travel agencies. James Henry Ewer died in October 1979.

578 (WLT 578G) was a Bristol LH; it was new in March 1969 and was passed to Orange in February 1972. It is seen here in a leafy location, *c.* 1970. (Ken Bateman: Andrew Mead Collection)

619 (JRK 619K), a Leyland/ Plaxton, poses for a Grey-Green publicity postcard by Stead Green Post Mill at Framlingham in Suffolk, during the summer of 1972. The postcard was available free of charge from Grey-Green travel offices during 1973 until stocks were depleted. (Grey-Green Coaches: Andrew Mead Collection)

630 (HJJ 630K) was purchased for the Birch fleet in July 1972. However it entered service with Grey-Green and only lasted a short while before passing to one of the Ewer dealerships. It is seen on the forecourt of No. 53 Stamford Hill. (Wilf Rowley: Owen Woodliffe Collection)

695 (MUL 695P) was a Bedford Duple. It is parked outside Ipswich garage in St Martin's Plain in late 1976. (Owen Woodliffe)

741 (SYU 741S) lays over in Swanage station coach park while on a tour to the Dorset town on 6 August 1978. The coach stands across the former platforms and track beds. The branch line closed in early January 1972. The redundant track was lifted and then taken away by British Road Services during July and August 1972. Swanage Urban District Council purchased the station in March 1974 from British Railways, and the track beds and goods yards were levelled. Thankfully the area has since been fully restored by Swanage Railway. (Bill Mead: Andrew Mead Collection)

757 (VYU 757S), a
Bedford with a Duple
body, was captured
leaving a June Derby
day. It was captured
negotiating the
temporary Metropolitan
Police signs at Tattenham
Corner, *c.* 1980.
(Phil Moth)

786 (YYL 786T) poses on
Westminster Bridge for
a Grey-Green publicity
shot with the dummy
vehicle registration 'YYL
790V'. This was one of
three coaches to receive
an experimental livery
during 1979. Behind
786 is the Palace of
Westminster, designed by
Augustus Pugin in 1846,
and to the right is the
Elizabeth Tower, named
in 2012, which houses
the 13.5-ton bell known
as 'Big Ben'. (Grey-Green
Coaches: Andrew
Mead Collection)

721 (RYL 721R), a
Bedford / Duple, was
one of three coaches to
receive an experimental
livery in 1979. It is
seen when about to
depart from Victoria
coach station on an
East Anglian Express
service on 23 April 1979.
(Andrew Mead)

2

Vehicle Fleet Numbers

Vehicle fleet numbering was introduced during the mid-1950s for most new vehicles entering the fleets of the George Ewer Group, through allocating consecutive vehicle registration numbers. Fleet numbers were not displayed on the vehicles except on the bus fleet from October 1987, with most service vehicles following a few years later. With regard to coaches it was practice to display the number in the three-track route number blinds in the later years, when the coach was not employed on a service route.

Haulage Vehicles

It is known that at least one Ford van purchased in 1932 carried a fleet number on the side of the vehicle. It was allocated fleet number 40 and was registered YY 1482. Some of the fleet had been allocated numbers on paper in the late 1940s. From December 1954, most new vehicles for the haulage and van fleet were allocated fleet numbers, commencing with No. 140. However, the practice of allocating numbers to this fleet was discontinued in September 1972 with No. 227 (MHX 227L), a Bedford TK 5-ton van, and further purchases were referred to by their random vehicle registration numbers. The last was purchased in April 1979, which was EDX 42T, a Bedford TK 3-ton van.

Single-Deck Coaches and Buses

Fleet numbers for the coaches were introduced in January 1956, commencing with the No. 301; however, No. 300 arrived in March. From that time all new coaches were numbered in a common sequence for all subsidiary coach companies. This sequence remained in use until the last new single-decker bus arrived in November 1998, which was numbered 983. Prior to 1956 all vehicles were known by their random vehicle registration numbers and this remained the case for most of the coaches acquired with takeovers, as well as odd used acquisitions. Acquired used single-deck buses were numbered in the 8xx series (801–808 and 814–819), using fleet numbers previously allocated to coaches.

Sixteen Plaxton-bodied coaches went to East Lancs body builders for re-bodying into buses in 1992. In this view a Volvo B10M chassis, which is either 855 (A855 UYM) or 856 (A856 UYM), waits for its new bus body to be fitted. (David Barrow)

Re-bodied 856 (A856 UYM) is seen at Chingford bus station while on route 179 – and not 313 as shown! –on 9 September 1995. (Andrew Mead)

Double-Deck Coaches and Buses

The first double-deck vehicle was acquired in August 1976, having previously been operated by Whippet Coaches. It was registered KCH 106 and so it was decided to number the double-deck fleet in the 1xx series. However, 106 was in fact the only used example to be numbered in the 1xx series, which was later reserved for new double-deck coaches and buses.

Later additions received numbers previously allocated to the haulage vehicle fleet. Coaches were numbered 101–105, 107–108, and buses were numbered 109–161, 163–168, 170–172 and 178–183. Numbers 163–168 and 170–172 were rebodied from single-deck coaches 863–868 and 870–872 and so therefore renumbered into the double-deck fleet.

All other acquired used double-deck buses were numbered in the 4xx, 5xx and later the 7xx series, again using previously allocated fleet numbers to earlier coaches.

Leyland PD2 106 (KCH 106) attended the London Bus Rally at Brockwell Park on 8 July 1979. Here it carries its first Grey-Green livery. (Andrew Mead)

106 (KCH 106), wearing its second Grey-Green livery, picks up passengers outside the Odeon cinema at Muswell Hill while taking part in the Odeon Muswell Hill Routemaster Bus Rally on 23 March 1984. The Odeon became the Everyman Cinema during the summer of 2015. (Andrew Mead)

Former 106 (KCH 106 – now XMD 47A) is seen parked at Southampton City Transport Portswood depot in around May 1991, after disposal from Grey-Green and before being acquired by Maybury's Big Bus Company in June 1991. In this view, 106 carries its third Grey-Green livery. (Brian Botley)

Former Leyland 106 (KCH 106 – now XMD 47A) is now in the ownership of the Big Bus Company. It waits outside the 'Girl Guides' shop at Nos 17–19 Buckingham Palace Road during May 1992 while on a sightseeing tour of London. The Big Bus Company was formed in June 1991 by brother and sister Richard and Ellenor Maybury. 106 was one of the first buses in the Big Bus Company fleet along with a former vintage East Kent vehicle; many staff joined the company from rival operator London Cityrama. Their father Brian and half-sister Lesley Maybury owned rival operator London Sightseeing Tours before selling out to Ensign Bus, who merged it into their 'London Pride' sightseeing operation. Brian Maybury had originally operated in Dorset. (Syd Tombleson)

166, formerly 866 (B866 XYR) and previously fitted with a Plaxton coach body, poses for the camera near to the East Lancs body works in February 1992. Note the three-track black-on-yellow route number blinds at the side, which were previously fitted in the coach destination display. (David Barrow)

Engineering and Support Vehicles

From August 1992, crew-change, service and some training vehicles that had diesel engines were numbered in the 0xx series. Some crew-change vehicles had previously carried a two-digit running number for a very short period. Numbers 011–019 were allocated to vehicles in the Engineers' Dept.; 021–027 were allocated to small crew-change vehicles; and 031 onwards were allocated to larger crew-change vehicles. Crew-change vehicles with petrol engines were not allocated fleet numbers.

Ford Escort estate car VOY 737M is seen at the Grey-Green-sponsored London Bus Rally at Brockwell Park on 22 July 1978. The car did not have a fleet number and was allocated to the publicity department. It was the only car to carry the Grey-Green name and livery. The car was at the end of its Grey-Green life when this picture was captured. To the left are London Transport LS200 (THX 200S), Grey-Green 764 (XYK 764T) and 760 (XYK 760T). (Phil Moth)

This unregistered ex-War Department Thornycroft 'Big Ben' recovery vehicle was transferred from Ewer dealer T. H. Nice of Bury St Edmunds in 1970. It operated on Ewer-owned trade plates '204 CF'. It is parked on the forecourt of No. 55 Stamford Hill. (Wilf Rowley: Owen Woodliffe Collection)

Bedford CF drop-side truck SPV 723R was new in April 1977 and allocated to the Engineering Dept. at Stamford Hill. It was not allocated a fleet number. It is seen here at the Grey-Green-sponsored London Bus Rally, part of the Lambeth Country Show, at Brockwell Park, Herne Hill, on 22 July 1979. (Andrew Mead)

012 (E415 ATN), new in August 1987, was a Ford Transit van allocated to the Engineers Dept. and was painted in this striking coach-style livery. It is seen inside the main garage at No. 55 Stamford Hill on 22 October 1992. (Andrew Mead)

017 (M984 WES), new in April 1995, was one of a small number of Land Rovers owned over the last few years of operation. It was allocated to the Engineering Dept. and was in general driven by Ron Barnard. It is seen leaving the workshops and crossing the forecourt on its way to assist a vehicle during the mid-1990s. (Andrew Mead)

043 (D611 JPW) was a used example of a crew-change Ford Transit personnel carrier, acquired in November 1994. It is seen at South End Green route 24 terminus on 5 March 1995. (Andrew Mead)

Summary

The 2xx series was never used to number passenger vehicles, while the 3xx and 6xx series were only used once to number coaches.

However, just to confuse everyone, the 2xx and the 3xx series were used on the DAF Alexander double-deck 'DLA' class buses, which were temporarily transferred from Arriva London. For the record, these were: 238–247 (S238 JUA–S247 JUA) and 297–315 (T297 FGN–T299 FGN, T110 GGO and T301 FGN–T315 FGN). Their fleet numbers were also known as DLA 38–DLA47 and DLA 97–DLA115.

Therefore, during the last few years of the company, the following fleet number sequences were all in use together: 0xx (engineering and support); 1xx (new double-deck coaches and buses); 2xx and 3xx (loaned double-deck buses); 4xx, 5xx and 7xx (used double-deck buses); 8xx and 9xx (new and used single-deck coaches and buses).

314 (T314 FGN) lays over at North Greenwich station while on route 188, before heading off to Euston on 9 April 2000. (Andrew Mead)

3

The 1980s –
The Penultimate Decade

807 (EYH 807V) picks up passengers at Swanage bus and railway station on 20 August 1983 while on route 181, which operated between Romford and Weymouth jointly with Eastern National Omnibus Company during that summer. (Andrew Mead)

819 (FYX 819W) waits to pick up passengers in Shore Road, Swanage, after a day tour to the Dorset seaside town on 16 August 1984. (Andrew Mead)

814 (FYX 814W) picks up a handful of passengers from outside the East Kent Road Car Co. booking office at The Parade, Margate, on the 18.00 departure Kent Coast Express, on 25 May 1981. (Andrew Mead)

In this busy scene at Tattenham Corner during the late 1980s to early 1990s, we see Leyland 843 (PYE 843Y) queuing to leave the Epsom Downs racecourse on a June Derby day. To the left are stacks of temporary Metropolitan Police traffic signs, which remind us of the time when the police controlled the traffic at all of London's major events. (Phil Moth)

883 (D883 FYL) is seen just after delivery in March 1987 on the forecourt of 55 Stamford Hill. It was part of a batch of six, all fitted with Plaxton bodywork. 866 (B866 XYR) is just visible to the rear. (Ken Bateman: Andrew Mead Collection)

Volvo/Duple 894 (E894 KYW) stands on the forecourt of No. 55 Stamford Hill in October 1988. The coach was later stolen from an Essex outstation and not recovered. (Jim Blake)

The Changes Commence

The decade started with the winding up of World Wide Coaches Ltd on 1 January. Their Plough Lane yard in Wimbledon was sold and the remaining coaches were transferred to Nos 2–7 Angel Road, Edmonton, as a separate unit within Grey-Green. The Mile End garage closed on 9 March.

To create extra space for coach parking, demolition work commenced on the Victorian house at No. 55 Stamford Hill during late April 1980. It had been used by the company for fifty years, but had largely been disused over the past few months.

The house at No. 55 Stamford Hill, captured on 8 April 1980, just a few days before it was demolished. 789 (YYL 789T) rests to the left while, on the right, just visible is 618 (JRK 618K). (Bill Mead: Andrew Mead Collection)

Grey-Green Travel, who had operated the travel office, moved into a mobile cabin situated on the forecourt, which remained in use until 1 March 1985.

Cowie Takes Over the Driving

The George Ewer Group was acquired by Sunderland-based motor dealer T. Cowie Ltd in June 1980. Tom Cowie then took over from Henry George Ewer as chairman of George Ewer & Co. Ltd, while Andrew Cowie became managing director. Tom Cowie had become company secretary of his father's second-hand motorcycle business at the age of sixteen in December 1938. He entered into the car dealership in Sunderland during September 1962 and, on 31 December 1964, the firm became a public limited company. The motorcycle business ceased during 1978. Tom Cowie received the OBE in 1982 and was knighted in 1992.

The Cowie Group purchased coach dealer and distributor Hughes Daf Ltd of Cleckheaton, near Leeds, in September 1988. The firm had been established in 1946 and, at the time of takeover, supplied 93 per cent of all new Daf coaches with Duple and Plaxton bodies to operators in Great Britain, as well as supplying Daf coaches with Van Hool bodies to operators on the Continent. Previously during mid-1987, the Cowie Group had purchased motor dealer Keith & Boyle who, of course, were the owners of Orange Luxury Coaches until October 1953, when they sold the firm to the George Ewer Group.

The Vans Arrive at the End of the Road

The haulage fleet was wound up during September 1980. The last van was disposed of by July 1981, which had been retained for use on a contract. This brought to a very sad end ninety-five years of goods transportation, which at one time had been a major part of the George Ewer operation. During the Second World War, the haulage fleet was located at No. 2a Forest Road, Dalston, London, E8, where the operation remained until the 1960s. At this time during the early 1960s, the drivers wore long grey coats with black uniform caps. The vans then moved to the former Fallowfield & Britten premises at Nos 387–393 Bethnal Green Road, Shoreditch, London, E2. In 1971 there were forty-two vans and five tankers operating in the haulage fleet, which comprised Bedford, Ford, Morris and Scammell marques. The five Scammell Routeman tankers, numbered 167–171 (161–171 AUW), were purchased in 1960 and 1961 for a Shell-Mex contract to collect and deliver heating oil. Two were based at Stamford Hill, while the others were based at Northfleet in Kent. One of the regular tanker drivers was Ken Talbot, who drove tours on Sundays. The haulage fleet moved during late 1978 to No. 345 Mile End Road, Mile End, London, E1, and some were garaged in the former Classique Coaches garage at No. 479 Lea Bridge Road, Leyton, London, E10. Although the haulage was disposed of by 1981, vans continued to form an important part of the Grey-Green fleet throughout the 1990s, being used as crew-change vehicles for the bus routes.

168 (168 AUW) was a
Scammell Routemen
tanker, and was part of
a batch of five, 167–71,
new in 1960/1. It is
seen on the forecourt
of No. 53 Stamford
Hill during the 1960s.
(Wilf Rowley: Owen
Woodliffe Collection)

Two of the remaining
Bedford TK vans from
the haulage fleet are
here in withdrawn
condition and await their
future when seen on the
forecourt of Edmonton
garage on 8 April 1980.
Looking rather sorry for
themselves, on the left is
217 (EMK 217J), while
next to it is NCF 780G.
(Andrew Mead)

024 (F471 XOG), new
in August 1988, was a
Ford Escort van supplied
by one of the Cowie
dealerships for use on
'crew changes'. It is seen
parked at Barking garage
on 19 September 1993.
(Andrew Mead)

British Coachways fly into Action

During late September 1980, it was announced that Grey-Green and Wallace Arnold of Leeds were to operate a network of express coach routes, 'British Coachways', as an alternative to the two state-owned bus groups – the National Bus Company, who operated National Express and the Scottish Bus Group – with a consortium of other independent coach operators. Immediately after deregulation of coach services, British Coachways was launched on Monday 6 October 1980 at the King's Cross coach terminal (or the London coach station, as it was known) in Euston Road by Norman Fowler, who at the time was Secretary of State for Transport. The coach terminal had been opened on 14 May 1980 by Grey-Green on behalf of PSV Operators Ltd on the site of the former London Midland Railway Somers Town goods yard, which British Rail closed in 1975, becoming a temporary car park. Of interest, it was decided at the eleventh hour on Saturday 19 July 1980 to hold the Grey-Green-sponsored London Bus Rally on this site the following day, as its designated site in Brockwell Park in Herne Hill, London, SE24, had become waterlogged due to severe inclement weather during the show on the Saturday. The Grey-Green-designed British Coachways livery was white with red and blue stripes swept upwards towards the rear. Other operators who joined the consortium at the start were Ellerman-Beeline of Middlesbrough, Morris Bros. of Swansea, Parks of Hamilton and Shearings of Altrincham. Within a few weeks, further operators came into the group, who included Barton Transport of Nottingham, Excelsior of Bournemouth, Warner-Farfax of Bristol and York Bros of

771 (YYL 771T) was repainted into Grey-Green-designed British Coachways livery at No. 53 Stamford Hill during September 1980. It carried dummy vehicle registration number 'SYH 800W' in company publicity photographs. It is seen here just after leaving the paint shop, minus its windscreen wipers, before it entered service on British Coachways routes after 6 October 1980. (Grey-Green Coaches: Andrew Mead Collection)

Northampton. Grey-Green withdrew from British Coachways on 1 July 1981, due to financial losses. The charting was then taken over by Wallace Arnold at their Evan Evans Coaches King's Cross depot in York Way. British Coachways sadly folded on 18 October 1982; however, some remaining operators continued services under their own names. The British Library has since been built on the King's Cross coach terminal site. The livery design was retained by Grey-Green after pulling out of the consortium. The three remaining Cowie coaching units adopted the livery as follows: the basic colour was white, as it was with British Coachways, while the flag design varied in colour. Grey-Green were green and orange; Dix Travel were brown and orange; and World Wide were blue and orange. The orange colour was a reminder of the old Orange Luxury Coaches livery.

A Seed was Sown in the Garden of England

Following the withdrawal from British Coachways, Grey-Green had a number of spare coaches, and so these were hired to Olsen Brothers of Strood for their Kent Commuter services into Central London. Grey-Green took over some of Olsen's routes during January 1982, which were to form the start of the Kent operations, lasting until the end of April 1996. The first Kent depot, a yard of an acre in size, was acquired by the side of the River Medway in Knight's Place, Strood, in May 1986. Richard Davey became the Kent Division Manager. Office accommodation was the former mobile cabin that had stood on the forecourt of Nos 53–55 Stamford Hill, which had been unused for the past fourteen months. Previously, drivers took their coaches home or they were parked at the Tollgate Services on the A2. During 1986–1988 a programme of day tours were operated with local Medway pick-up points.

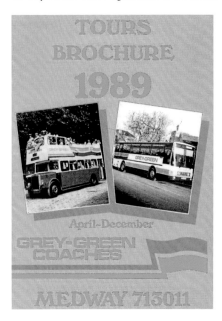

The cover of the 1989 Kent tours brochure. (Andrew Mead Collection)

On the Move

Dix Luxury Coaches moved from their rented yard at Heath Garage, Wood Lane, in Becontree Heath during August 1982 into new premises at Heathway Industrial Estate, Manchester Way, Wantz Road in Dagenham. Their travel office remained open in Wood Lane. The Edmonton coach station, which was situated at Nos 2–7 Angel Road, Edmonton, London, N18, closed in 1984. It had been opened in 1952 by the Mayor of Edmonton. During its last months it was home to World Wide Coaches. The premises were taken over by the tyre retailer Kwik Fit. In 1994 the former garage and Grey-Green Travel office were demolished to make way for the widening of the North Circular Road (A406).

The old Edmonton garage at Angel Road, just before demolition on 30 January 1994. (Andrew Mead)

The second 801 in the fleet was a former demonstrator acquired from Leyland in May 1984 and was then allocated to the Dix fleet. It was registered FRN 801W. It is seen on the forecourt of No. 55 Stamford Hill in the summer of 1983, while on loan from Leyland Motors. (Paul Bateson)

839 (A839 SYR) was
one of six Leyland
Royal Tigers with Roe
Doyen bodies ordered.
However only one was
delivered, which was
in September 1983.
It rest on Stamford
Hill forecourt.
(Paul Bateson)

872 (B872 XYR) shows
off its Dagenham name
and telephone number
when seen at the
depot on 1 April 1990.
(Andrew Mead)

878 (D878 FYL) was
the last coach to carry
the Dix Travel name and
livery. (Brian Pask)

878 is seen, having been repainted into Grey-Green livery, at the Wantz Road depot at Dagenham on 21 September 1991. However the Dix Travel name is still displayed on the destination blind. The coach was later lost in an overnight arson attack at Dunmow in November 1993, after being stolen from its Essex commuter outstation. (Andrew Mead)

Coach Operations on the Decline

Grey-Green pulled out of the East Anglian Express (EAX) services pool after 24 February 1985. Grey-Green had been associated with the services since 1928. During 1968 the routes were pooled with Eastern National and Eastern Counties, and operated from Victoria coach station to major towns in East Anglia. Various National Bus Company operators took over Grey-Green's former routes, including Green Line.

The summer tours programme started to decline during 1985 and Enfield operator Oakfield Tours Ltd, trading as Enfieldian Tours, increased their tours programme to compensate for this. Summer 1987 was the final year of the coastal express services.

Assisting the Police …

Throughout the 1980s Grey-Green had contracts to provide coaches with many large companies and organisations. A contract that had been acquired on the purchase of Dix Luxury Coaches in February 1976 was for the Ford Motor Company in Dagenham, which was the reason why Dix continued to operate mainly Ford coaches. One of the more interesting clients was the Metropolitan Police. Generally coaches were provided to transport serials of police officers into Central London for ceremonial events and to maintain public order. At busy times many coaches were hired from other operators, which included BTS of Borehamwood and Horseshoe Coaches of Tottenham. Former driver John Wilks remembers seeing groups of police officers push starting a coach operated by Continental Pioneer of Richmond! Most weekends it was a common sight to see coaches parked in the vicinity of St James's Park Underground station while their passengers were fed at either New Scotland Yard or at other 'Met' premises a stone's throw away at No. 58 Buckingham Gate, London, SW1. These were built in the nineteenth century and were the former army headquarters of the Queen's Westminster Rifles regiment. At the time the Metropolitan Police owned around fifty Bedford buses and coaches, mostly with Duple and Lex bodywork, which were stabled at their Central Transport Garage in Lambeth Road. They were later replaced by a batch of Dennis Darts with East Lancs bodies.

Metropolitan Police traffic patrol car NYX 14Y, a Rover SD1, takes a break at Leicester Forest services on the M1 while escorting at least eight coaches full of Metropolitan Police officers and twenty police Ford Transit carriers to RAF Dishforth in North Yorkshire, on 28 October 1984 to help the local forces police the miners' strike. At the rear, Leyland 807 (EYH 807V) rests with Hardings of Betchworth NPK 211W. (Owen Woodliffe)

World Wide 711 (SYU 711S), a Leyland Leopard with a Plaxton body, gets ready to leave Battersea park with a serial of police officers after the Easter parade on 6 April 1980. (Andrew Mead)

London Bus Services

During December 1985 Grey-Green commenced bidding for various London Regional Transport (LRT)-tendered London bus routes. After a period of almost a year, Grey-Green was successful and was awarded its first tender. It was the No. 173, which operated between Stratford and Becontree Heath. Ten Daimler Fleetlines were acquired in November 1986 from Essex dealer Ensign Bus, which were former South Yorkshire Passenger Transport Executive buses. They were prepared for service at the Stamford Hill workshops for the launch of the service on 28 February 1987. It was decided to give them the trading name of 'EastenderBus' and they were painted in the Dix colours of white, brown and orange. They were based at the Dix Travel depot at Wantz Road. The covered premises next-door had been acquired to accommodate the buses and the dividing wall was removed. Running numbers were carried in holders fitted on the front off-side of the bus. Garage code 'DX' was allocated by LRT to the Dix Travel depot. Grey-Green's own radio system was installed on the buses instead of using LRT's CentreComm network.

Other LRT-tendered bus routes quickly followed on 17 October of that year; these were the 179 (Barking–Chingford) and 379 (Chingford town service). These were also operated from the Dix Travel depot; however, it was now decided to use the 'Grey-Green' name on all buses and so the 'EastenderBus' name was phased out. More buses were acquired for these routes and were painted in the same colour scheme. However, they carried an orange-coloured Grey-Green name. Fleet numbers were now introduced for the bus fleet, as some registration number numerals were duplicated. In just under a month, the LRT route 125 between Winchmore Hill and North Finchley commenced operation from Stamford Hill. LRT allocated the garage code 'GG' to Stamford Hill. However neither of the two garage codes were ever overtly displayed.

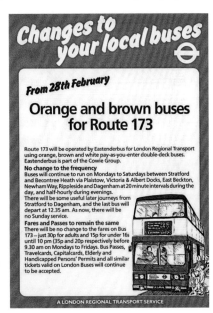

Front cover of LRT route 173 publicity leaflet, issued in February 1987. This was Grey-Green's first LRT route, which commenced on 28 February 1987. (Andrew Mead Collection)

Inside the Wantz Road 'EastenderBus' (Dix Travel) on 28 February 1987 are, from left to right, 528 (OKW 528R), 506 (OKW 506R) and 528 (OKW 528R). They were purchased in November 1986 for route 173 and painted at Stamford Hill. (Andrew Mead)

124 (F124 PHM) collects passengers in Oakleigh Road, Whetstone, London, N20, while on route 125 to Winchmore Hill on 27 June 1993. (Andrew Mead)

Scania demonstrator E200 WHS was loaned to Grey-Green between 6 and 29 February 1988. It operated on route 125 in the colours of Scottish operator A1 Services. It is seen here on a Sunday service having just left Little Park Gardens bus terminus in Enfield for North Finchley. Trinity Church is to the rear. (Brian Pask)

404 (H104 GEV) and 120 (F120 PHM) on the forecourt outside 55 Stamford Hill. 404 was waiting for some attention in the workshop on 24 April 1993. This was taken from the old 'Board Room' window inside No. 53. (Andrew Mead)

Industrial action at London Country North East Ltd resulted in interesting developments in early February 1988, when routes 298 and 313 were operated on a temporary basis for a few days using coaches from Dagenham and Stamford Hill depots. Fares were not charged; however, 'honesty boxes', which were old Gibson ticket machine boxes with a slot cut in top and sited by the driver, were used for fare collection. A 'Gibson' ticket machine was at hand should a passenger request a bus ticket. The routes were completely taken over from 22 February.

News soon followed that the company had won the prestigious route 24, which operated between South End Green in Hampstead Heath (adjacent to the now famous Royal Free London NHS Hospital) and Grosvenor Road in Pimlico, passing famous central London landmarks such as Trafalgar Square, Horse Guards Parade, Downing Street, Palace of Westminster, Westminster Abbey and Westminster School for Boys. It was the first Central London-tendered bus route to be awarded to an independent operator. It was decided to have a completely new livery for this route, one which was more appropriate to its name: Grey-Green. Livery experiments were carried out on existing buses. The livery of grey and green with an orange stripe was designed by Ray Stening of 'Best Impressions'. Thirty Volvo D10M Citybuses with Alexander bodywork were numbered 115–144 (F115–144 PHM) were purchased for the route. Worthy of mention here is a note of related interest about the northern terminus at South End Green. The London Street Tramways Company had constructed a terminus by 1887 for their horse-drawn trams at the same location at the junction of Pond Street for visitors to Hampstead Heath. Around six years later a shelter was built at the terminus for the tramway men and remains in use today for bus drivers of routes 24 and 168. Their horse stables and tram depot were around 400 yards away in Cressy Road and, after much rebuilding, were closed by the London Transport Executive (LTE) in 1949. After this, it was transferred to British Road Services Ltd for use as a general-haulage depot (depot code 'CJ'), which, like LTE, was a subsidiary of the British Transport Commission that had been formed on 1 January 1948. In 1897 underground public toilets were constructed for use by the many tramway passengers visiting the popular location. The now-listed London Borough of Camden Victorian conveniences remain open to the public with little alteration since the first opening.

814 (FYX 814W) is seen on temporary operation of LRT route 298 at Cockfosters station in February 1988. (Tony Wilson)

888 (E888 KYW) waits at Potter Bar station while operating the temporary 313 route to Chingford station in February 1988. (Bill Mead: Andrew Mead Collection)

Former coach 105 (E105 JYV) collects passengers in Church Street, Enfield, while on route 313 to Chingford on 8 September 1992. (Andrew Mead)

492 (GND 492N) is seen at the northern end terminal of the Piccadilly line outside Cockfosters station while on route 298 on 11 May 1990. (Andrew Mead)

455 (EWF 455V), still in acquired South Yorkshire livery, waits at Potters Bar station while on route 313 in *c.* 1988. (Tony Wilson)

Front cover of LRT route 24 publicity leaflet, issued during October 1988. The route commenced on 5 November 1988, 383 years after Guy Fawkes led the Gunpowder Plot to blow up the Houses of Parliament. (Andrew Mead Collection)

A Daimler Fleetline, XAK 348L, was acquired in March 1988 from West Yorkshire PTE for use as a driver trainer, mainly for route 24. It is seen inside the garage at No. 55 Stamford Hill. (Phil Moth)

104 (E104 JYV) overtakes 128 (F128 PHM) in Victoria Street on 17 May 1990. 104 had just departed from Bressenden Place on a Kent commuter journey, while 128 is on route 24. Number 104 was later converted for bus use and operated from Barking garage. (Andrew Mead)

117 (F117 PHM) is seen at the Pimlico terminus at the southern end of route 24. The King William IV public house is to the right. To the left is the chimney of the Western Pumping Station, which dates from 1875. (Tony Wilson)

134 (F134 PHM) and 117 (F117 PHM) wait at the northern end of route 24 at South End Green, Hampstead. (Tony Wilson)

During the morning of 7 February 1991, terrorists fired three mortar bombs at No. 10 Downing Street from a van parked nearby. This resulted in major road closures for the rest of the day. A snow storm later added to the chaos. A security alert at Victoria railway station meant that the easiest way for the author to reach Charing Cross was to trudge in the snow along The Mall through St James's Park from Buckingham Palace to Trafalgar Square. The sound of a Volvo B10M coming from behind and a ready camera resulted in this unique capture of 129 (F129 PHM) taking this very unauthorised shortcut, where buses are banned, en route to Hampstead Heath. The white buildings were designed by John Nash for the Prince Regent. (Andrew Mead)

Growth Blooms in the Garden of England

Grey-Green was keen to improve the facilities for the Kent operation and so a new depot was built on land at Maritime Way, Medway City Estate in Frindsbury on the outskirts of Strood. It consisted of the drivers' room, offices and workshops. It became part operational on 13 September 1988 and fully operational from 28 September. In October 1989 Grey-Green commenced the operation of their first Kent County Council-tendered bus route.

868 (B868 XYR) takes a wash at the Kent depot on 22 January 1989. (Paul Bateson)

The Kent depot at Frindsbury, near Strood, in 1992. (Andrew Mead)

An extra Leyland National was acquired from County Bus & Coach as a non-runner for spare parts. It was registered LPB 208P but was not allocated a Grey-Green fleet number. It is seen on 3 April 1993 'dumped' at the Kent depot, where it spent all of its life with Grey-Green without moving. The remains of scrapped Metrobus 451 (EWF 451V) are just visible to the left. (Andrew Mead)

Paul Shepherd drives 808 (UPB 296S) out of Maidstone Chequers bus station while on Kent County Council's Saturday-only route 130 to Twydall on 6 February 1993. (Andrew Mead)

886 (E886 KYW), driven by Paul Shepherd, passes through the High Street in Rainham while on Kent route 130 to Twydall on 27 March 1995. (Andrew≈Mead)

875 (C875 CYX), driven by Paul Shepherd, covers a meal-time relief on Kent County Council route 130 and is seen leaving Maidstone Chequers bus station on 3 April 1993. Note the Ewer on hire label in the destination aperture. (Andrew Mead)

802 (D102 NDW) was one of three used Lynxes acquired from Merthyr Tydfil for use on Kent routes. It is seen here on route 142 at Chatham on 10 September 1994. Visible to the rear is 886 (E886 KYW), on route 150. (Andrew Mead)

806 (NPK 229R), along with four others, were acquired from County Bus in March 1992 for use on Kent routes. It is seen here still in County Bus livery with 'Grey-Green' names on route 151 at West Malling Airfield Estate on 7 April 1992. The destination is displayed on the specially made rear-style registration plate. (Andrew Mead)

Maintenance problems caused the South Eastern Traffic Commissioner to revoke the local service licences of an Isle of Sheppy operator. Grey-Green and Smith's of Sittingbourne took over the operator's Kent County Council-tendered bus routes. Here we see 818 (FYX 818W) posing in Bridge Road, Sheerness, by the Maidstone & District garage while on route 367 before departing to Wealden Point on 27 January 1990. (Andrew Mead)

Former Manchester 510 (GNC 288N), acquired in August 1987, is seen at the Kent depot before leaving for commercial route 814, which operated between Hoo and Lordswood via Rochester School. The short-lived route was operated from 4 September to 25 October 1989. (Owen Woodliffe)

804 (LPB 203P) passes through Hempstead Valley shopping centre while on the Saturday Maidstone–Twydall route 130, c. 1995. (Paul Gooderson)

864 (B864 XYR) waits to be loaded with beer and other goods while in the coach park of the 'Auchan' hypermarket on the outskirts of Boulogne in France while on an excursion from Medway in June 1986. (Owen Woodliffe)

946 (M946 LYR) waits along Victoria Embankment before starting a Kent commuter service from Victoria on 20 March 1995. Visible behind the front view is the turbine steamer *Queen Mary*, which was built for services in the Clyde in 1933 and is seen here in the ownership of Bass Charrington as a restaurant. On the rear view of 946 the 'Medway' name and telephone number are clearly visible. (Andrew Mead)

Coaches were often hired from other operators to cover Kent commuter services. Former 862 (B862 XYR), seen here with Bradley of London, E10, still wears its Grey-Green livery. It is covering a Kent commuter working on route 803 to the Medway towns. It pulls away from the Embankment stop at Charing Cross on 15 July 1992. This vehicle and 869 were sold before the rest of the batch went for rebodying to become buses. (Andrew Mead)

A vehicle excise licence (or tax disc) from former 862 (B862 XYR) while in the ownership of Bradley, London, E10. The tax disc was phased out during 2015. (Andrew Mead Collection)

A tip-off from one of the Kent drivers during the day on 22 May 1992 informed the author that a Barking-based bus was to operate on an afternoon departure on one of the Kent commuter routes to the Medway towns. It therefore resulted in the author waiting for it to arrive at the Victoria Embankment coach stop by Hungerford Railway Bridge for a while. Alas, the destination blind had jammed, showing LRT route destination 'Loughton Station'. However, the correct route number – 807 – was displayed on this semi-posed photo of 826 (J826 CYL). It was collected by Barking staff from the Kent depot overnight. (Andrew Mead)

104 (E104 JYV) now converted for LRT bus work, along with sister 105, operates a homeward bound Kent commuter journey on the 24 February 1992. It is seen here at Victoria Embankment while on route 805 before destination blinds were fitted. (Andrew Mead)

Persistent parking by coaches in LRT's bus stands outside the Apollo Theatre (formally the Gaumont British New Victoria Cinema) in Vauxhall Bridge Road, Victoria, resulted in LRT complaining to the Metropolitan Police for extra enforcement of that area. So, here we see Kent-based 896 (E896 KYW) fitted with a wheel-clamp! (It was one of only six coach wheel clamps owned by the 'Met' at that time.) It had been left unattended while the driver went to get a cup of tea before departure from Bressenden Place to the Medway towns. The result threw some of the afternoon commuter departures into disarray on 26 May 1989. (Andrew Mead)

4

The 1990s – The Final Years

More London-tendered bus routes were acquired and more new buses were purchased to operate the routes; and so the bus fleet grew.

On Sunday 2 December 1990 the Kent depot at Strood held an open day for the general public. Money was raised for local charities. Many vehicles were on display and included at least two that had been brought from Stamford Hill, which included open-top bus 106.

A rapid sprint by the author enabled him to capture this un-posed view of a member of 'The Company of Pikemen and Musketeers' disembarking from 899 (E899 KYW) in North Carriage Drive in Hyde Park on 8 May 1995. They were taking part in VE Day fiftieth anniversary celebrations. The company was formed in 1925 and is the ceremonial unit of the Honourable Artillery Company; its members wear 1640s-style uniforms. (Andrew Mead)

916 (H916 XYT) is captured in Golders Green bus station while on LRT route 210 to Brent Cross shopping centre during the summer of 1997. The '79' running number plate is clearly visible, and is coloured blue, indicating a single-decker route due to the low-bridge in Stroud Green Road at Finsbury Park station. However, the odd double-decker did appear on the 210 route, which included 136 (F136 PHM) – it lost its roof under the bridge! (Bill Mead: Andrew Mead Collection)

116 (F116 PHM) waits at the terminus of the Saturday-only LRT route D9 at Crossharbour on 20 March 1993 before departing for the Bank in the City of London. (Andrew Mead)

407 (H107 GEV) was one of a batch acquired from County Bus with route 103 in January 1991. It is seen at Walthamstow while at work on route 275 on 11 April 1993. (Andrew Mead)

Former Newport 472 (DTG 372V) is seen at Walthamstow while on route 275. (Andrew Mead)

107 (E107 JYV) poses at Barking depot on 3 October 1993. New in December 1987 as a coach, it was transferred to the bus fleet for work on LRT routes from Barking depot. (Andrew Mead)

495 (GND 506N) was transferred from Stamford Hill to Dagenham for the temporary operation of route 252 which ran between Gidea Park and Collier Row from September to November 1988. 495 waits at Dagenham depot in September 1988. (Tom Townsin: Owen Woodliffe Collection)

Former Southampton Citybus Leyland Olympian 479 (279 ROW) poses at Barking depot in the sun on 3 October 1993. (Andrew Mead)

956 (P956 RUL) at
rest at Walthamstow
bus station while
operating on route
20 on 9 January 1999.
(Andrew Mead)

Single-doored 154
(G154 TYT) lays
over in Walthamstow
bus station while
on route 275 before
departure to Barking
on 9 January 1999.
(Andrew Mead)

Grey-Green, along
with Len Wright's
London Buslines,
covered route 123
between Tottenham
and Gants Hill for a
few days in July 1991.
Here 114 (E114 KYN)
lays over at Gants
Hill station on 28 July
1991. (Andrew Mead)

171, formerly coach 871 (B871 XYR), passes southbound over Waterloo Bridge while on route 188 to Greenwich in *c*. 1999. The bridge was designed by Sir Giles Gilbert Scott and opened in 1945. It was built mostly by a female workforce, and is sometimes referred to as 'The Ladies' Bridge'. (Tony Wilson)

In this posed line-up at the open day at the Kent depot, on 2 December 1990, are commuter coaches Scania 103 (C103 CYE), Scania 108 (E108 JYV) and Volvo bus 158 (H158 XYU). (Andrew Mead)

Dennis Dart 951 (M951 LYR) is seen on Kent route 126 to Maidstone outside Chatham Pentagon bus station in Military Road. It passes RM2217 (CUV 217C), owned by sister company South London Transport, which was operating on a special service to Chatham Dockyard as part of the VE Day fiftieth anniversary celebrations on 8 May 1995. (Andrew Mead)

On 6 January 1991, LRT route 103 and fourteen Leyland Olympian buses that operated on the route were taken over from Simco 314 Ltd, which had been formed out of part of County Bus & Coach Company. Somehow these buses were squashed into a now very cramped Dix Travel depot at Dagenham.

The increasing amount of LRT bus work meant that the Dix Travel depot at Wantz Road was now far too small from which to operate comfortably. In April 1992 a new depot was opened at No. 638 Ripple Road, Barking. The LRT garage code 'DX' was transferred to the new depot but still wasn't displayed on the buses at this stage. It is worth mentioning that Grey-Green had their own garage codes for internal use, which were: 'B' for Barking, 'K' for Strood in Kent and 'S' for Stamford Hill.

Cowie was eager to expand its London bus operation. During mid-1994, Cowie bid to purchase two of the London Buses operating subsidiary companies, which had been advertised for sale. These were Leaside Buses and London Northern. In September of that year it was confirmed that Cowie was successful in purchasing Leaside Buses Ltd from LRT-owned London Buses Ltd. The coach and commercial arm of Leaside Buses traded as Leaside Travel. The purchase of South London Transport Ltd soon followed. Both companies were quickly rebranded to 'Cowie Leaside' and 'Cowie South London'.

The Routes in the Garden were Pruned

On 1 May 1996 the Cowie Group disposed of the Kent depot at Strood, the Kent County Council bus routes, commuter coach routes and all the vehicles based there (twenty-one buses and coaches, and two service vehicles) with the exception of two Dennis Darts to the Pullman Group Ltd, owner of London Coaches (Kent) Ltd. The staff also transferred to London Coaches (Kent) Ltd. The Pullman Group also owned former London Buses subsidiary London Coaches Ltd, who at that time operated 'The Original London Sightseeing Tour' in central London. (The tour was originally started by the London Transport Executive during the summer of 1951 for the Festival of Britain celebrations. In December 1997, the tour was acquired by the Cowie Group and was sold in September 2014 to the French state-owned operator RAPT.) London Coaches (Kent) Ltd already had an established network of Kent commuter services, which operated between the Medway towns and the Green Line coach station at Bulleid Way in Victoria as part of the 'Green Line Associated Services' network. The Grey-Green name was quickly removed from all of the vehicles that had been acquired. Meanwhile the large 'Grey-Green' name, which donned the offices and workshop, was re-sited at the Barking depot, where it was to survive for the following two years. A start was made on repainting some of the coaches into the new owner's red livery, but was never completed. Eighteen days later the Kent County Council-tendered bus routes and the buses passed to local British Bus subsidiary Maidstone & District Motor Services Ltd. London Coaches Kent continued to operate commuter services from Maritime Way until 29 October 1999, when the depot was closed and remaining commuter routes passed to competitors Clarkes of London, SE26, and The Kings Ferry of Gillingham (The Kings Ferry was later acquired by National Express).

Also in 1996 Cowie purchased County Bus from the National Express Group. During August of that year, British Bus PLC was acquired, which included such companies as Green Line Travel and the dormant Shamrock & Rambler Coaches Ltd.

Former 802 (D102 NDW), now with London Coaches (Kent), operates the 130 route when seen in Maidstone during early May 1996. (Paul Gooderson)

Former 803 (D108 NDW), now numbered 3040 with Maidstone & District, picks up passengers outside Chatham bus station white on Kent route 142 on 24 May 1996. The Maidstone & District name is coloured cream and is placed on the orange band between the wheel arches. (Andrew Mead)

Former 902 (E902 MUC) with London Coaches (Kent) waits at the Green Line coach station in Buckingham Palace Road at stand 9 before departing to Medway on 25 July 1997. Stand 9 is now where Stagecoach's 'Oxford Tube' departs from, while stand 8, behind, is now the location from which Golden Tours 'Blue Route' Sightseeing Tour starts. Golden Tours acquired Frames Rickards Tours in 2001 and one of their former guides, Anthony, remains employed by Golden Tours. Stand 7, to the rear, is now occupied by Go-Ahead's X90 service to Oxford. (Andrew Mead)

(The original Shamrock & Rambler Motor Coaches had, of course, been associated with Orange Luxury Coaches.) Maidstone & District, along with its sister companies New Enterprise Coaches, Kentish Bus & Coach and Londonlinks, were also acquired with British Bus, bringing with it the former Grey-Green buses and routes it had acquired from London Coaches (Kent).

Arriva Arrives

A major decision was made during 1997 to rename the Cowie Group. The name chosen was 'Arriva'. Most of the Group's companies were given the Arriva branding from March 1998. Grey-Green Coaches Ltd had been renamed to Grey-Green Ltd during 1995 and on 2 April 1998 Grey-Green Ltd was renamed to Arriva London North East Ltd. Red Rover of Aylesbury, a dormant company that was part of Luton & District since 1987; it that had been acquired with British Bus PLC, and was then renamed to Grey-Green Ltd to protect the name. Meanwhile Leaside Buses Ltd was renamed to Arriva London North Ltd and South London Transport Ltd was renamed to Arriva London South Ltd.

131 (F131 PHM) waits in Walthamstow bus station on 9 January 1999 while on route 20. The 'Arriva' name is now carried, while the 'Grey-Green' name has been relocated next to the exit door. (Andrew Mead)

The forecourt of No. 55 Stamford Hill in 1995 with rebodied 167, formerly 867 (B867 XYR), facing the camera. (Andrew Mead)

A sorry-looking scene of the vacated Nos 53–55 Stamford Hill, as seen from a passing bus on 11 July 1998. (Andrew Mead)

It was a sad day on 27 March 1998, when the Grey-Green garage at No. 55 Stamford Hill closed after the buses had left for their day's work on the streets of London. The buses already carried the new Arriva 'wheels within wheels' logo. Their return later that day would be to the former Leaside bus garage, just a stone's throw away in Rookwood Road, which had garage code 'SF'. Numbers 53–55 Stamford Hill was sold. Number 55 was redeveloped, while No. 53 was subject to a Grade II preservation order.

Eurolines

Grey-Green's participation in the National Express Eurolines services to Amsterdam and Paris ceased at the end of August 1998. The coaches were then reallocated to other Arriva companies. The 'Eurolines' name had been in use since spring 1986. Grey-Green's long-term partner on the Amsterdam service since 1983 was Dutch coach operator Bovo Tours of Roelofarendsveen, the latter being a town just outside Amsterdam. After the collapse of 'Magic Bus' at Christmas 1982, Bovo Tours requested a partnership on the Amsterdam service. In 1983 Bovo Tours received a 25 per cent share, which was followed in 1984 by a 33 per cent share; the following year, it was increased again to a 50 per cent share of the service. Bovo Tours was established as a coach operator in December 1947 by two partners who had the family names of Boot and Voet. Fifty years later the company was being run by Voet's son and grandson. During the late 1990s they were operating around 140 coaches, which were maintained in their own workshops, and also ran a coach dealership. In 1996 they had acquired the small Amsterdam coach operator Labeto Reizen. In February 1997 Bovo Tours and fellow Dutch coach operator Oostenrijk of Diemen jointly acquired the Amsterdam coach tour operator Van Nood Reizen with each operator acquiring twelve coaches. Grey-Green was replaced on the Amsterdam service by KMP Coaches of Llanberis in north Wales. Grey-Green had originally commenced operation on Continental services in 1975.

This Mercedes Setra was one of the twelve coaches acquired by Bovo Tours in February 1997 with 50 per cent of Van Nood Reizen. 258 (BB-RT-96) was new to Van Nood in 1995. It is seen on 13 July 2001 while laying over at the New Covent Garden Market coach park at Vauxhall, having completed an overnight Eurolines service from Amsterdam to Victoria. (Andrew Mead)

This rear view of 932 (K932 VCP) clearly shows the various rear names. It is seen on 16 April 1993 passing St Martin-in-the-Fields Church, in Duncannon Street by Charing Cross railway station, on its return to Barking after completing a Eurolines service to Victoria. (Andrew Mead)

K547 RJX was one of a number of coaches loaned from Cowie dealer Huges-Daf to cover coach shortages. Here it leaves Victoria coach station and turns into Ebury Street on a Continental journey on the 24 June 1994. (Andrew Mead)

945 (M945 LYR), left, and 946 (M946 LYR) rest with 942 and 947, which are out of view, while their four drivers chat in this early morning view at Amstel station in Amsterdam on 28 March 1998. 945, 946 and 947 had just arrived on the overnight 142 service from Victoria, while 942 was about to depart on the 08.30 140 Eurolines service to Victoria. (Andrew Mead)

874 (C874 CYX) operates Essex commuter service 199 to Braintree when seen at Victoria Embankment in 1995. (Andrew Mead)

874 (C874 CYX) was the only coach to carry this experimental Cowie livery – thankfully! It is seen here in Millbank, London, SW1, near to the Tate Gallery, just before the 17.30 departure on Essex commuter service 199 on 6 March 1997. (Andrew Mead)

This Grey-Green coach stop flag dates from the mid to late 1950s and was sited by Chingford Green in Station Road, London, E4. It was photographed in early 1991 when Grey-Green's LRT routes 179, 313 and 379 passed by it. It was removed after almost forty years soon after this historic image was captured. (Andrew Mead)

The Essex Commuter routes and coaches were sold to a consortium of local Essex coach companies who called themselves Essex Express Ltd after the final departures on 2 October 1998.

During October, remaining coaches were transferred to other nearby Arriva operators, which included Arriva the Shires and Leaside Travel (the private hire and coaching arm of Arriva London North Ltd), who also took over the remaining contracts. The coach-based Edmonton depot of County Bus had been gradually merged with Leaside Travel, which continued to trade for a few further years. County Bus had acquired the remaining part of Sampson's Coaches from the Sampson family in 1989, who wanted to concentrate on their Broxbourne Zoo – now known as Paradise Wildlife Park. (Sampson's had previously operated buses for LRT in the Enfield area.) Oakfield Tours Ltd (Enfieldian Tours) of Enfield, owned by two former Grey-Green managers Peter Campling and John Harris, had previously acquired part of Sampson's Coaches in around 1987. Arriva decided to close Leaside Travel and dispose of the coaches. A new, short-lived, privately owned company emerged in February 2006 from Leaside Travel, which was named Roadways Travel Ltd of Edmonton, London, N9, and tried unsuccessfully to compete with Oakfield Tours.

891 (E891 KYW) passed within Arriva from County Bus (t/a Sampson's) to London Coaches at Wandsworth for use as a driver training vehicle. It is seen here on 4 June 1998 outside Wandsworth garage (garage code 'WD') with Enfieldian Tours driver John Froment, after passing his PSV driving test. (John Froment)

Former 892 (E892 KYW), now with Leaside Travel and seen re-registered with former RM1185, registration 185 CLT, waits at the Green Line coach station at Buckingham Palace Road before departing on the afternoon Green Line 711 service to Harlow during the summer of 1997. Bernard was the regular driver on this service and was always happy to have a chat about coaches, especially Elcock & Son of Ironbridge. (Andrew Mead)

Former 945 (M945 LYR), seen here with Arriva Cymru as their CDD945, leaves Marlborough Street bus station in Bristol in late 1998. (Ken Bateman: Andrew Mead Collection)

Former 949 (M949 LYR) was transferred to Arriva The Shires as their 4061. It waits to depart on Green Line route 797 from stand 7 at the Green Line coach station at Buckingham Palace Road, *c.* 1998. (Unknown: Andrew Mead Collection)

Former 927 (J927 CYL), having been transferred to Arriva East Herts & Essex as their 4337, lays over while on route 310A at Hertford bus station on 26 February 1999. (Andrew Mead)

Over the following two years, the remaining Grey-Green buses were repainted into Arriva London red livery and gradually obtained class prefix letters as part of the fleet number. All traces of Grey-Green had been eliminated by early 2000. On 27 August 2010, Arriva was acquired by the German state-owned railway operator Deutsche Bahn.

950 (M950 LYR) is minus its names, having recently returned from loan to Maidstone & District. It lays over in Walthamstow bus station while on route 20 on 29 January 2000. This was new to the Kent depot for Kent County Council routes in April 1995. (Andrew Mead)

VA116 (F116 PHM) now in Arriva London red livery operated the 125 route at Tally Ho Corner, North Finchley, on 28 December 1999. (Andrew Mead)

157 (H157 XYU), now with Arriva London, waits at the Battersea terminus, the southern end of LRT route 19 on 23 April 2000. (Syd Tombleson)

819 (L119 YVK) was transferred from Kentish Bus with route 225. It is seen in Molesworth Street in Lewisham on 29 August 1998 before departing to Rotherhithe. (Andrew Mead)

936 (L936 GYL) is seen here, now in Arriva London red livery, while on route 173 at East Becton District Centre on 8 July 2000. (Andrew Mead)

5

The After Life

The George Ewer Group and its successors have owned and operated well over 1,500 vehicles of various descriptions, and so it stands to reason that most will turn up somewhere in the country with subsequent operators for further use.

However, only a very small number are in preservation or semi-preservation. The Ewer Group Enthusiasts' Club attempted to preserve Harrington Wayfarer-bodied Leyland Tiger 331 (VGT 331) but, alas, the project failed and the coach was eventually scrapped. Probably the most famous bus in preservation is 106 (KCH 106,

A full-sized replica of the former 453 (ALR 453B) was created by artist Richard Wilson as part of the London 2012 Festival within the cultural Olympiad. The replica, which rocked up and down, is seen balanced on the roof of the De La Warr Pavilion in Bexhill on 24 July 2012. 453 played an important role in the 1969 film *The Italian Job* and is seen here in the colours with which it was painted in the film. (Tony Zotti, MBE)

Rochford Sports football club acquired former 522 (JUV 522D) in May 1988. It is seen at John H. Burrows Recreation Ground in nearby Hadleigh in April 1989. Rochford is near the towns of Rayleigh and Southend in Essex. (Owen Woodliffe)

Former 542 (JUV 542D) with G & S Travel (Rimmer) of Ramsgate, Kent, rests in its home overnight bay in Vere Road coach park, Broadstairs, on 26 May 1980. (Andrew Mead)

Former Dix Ford 738 (SYU 738S), seen here with Southgate & Finchley Coaches, leaves Wood Street and enters the High Street in Barnet, Herts, on 30 March 1993. (Andrew Mead)

Former 745 (XYK 745T) was acquired during mid-1988 by Pam Dobbins, who traded as 'Plan Ahead' of New Southgate, London, N11. It is seen her on 30 August 1992 at Margate in the former railway goods yards, which by that time had been converted into a coach park. (Andrew Mead)

Posed for the photographer is former 801 (CYH 801V), which had been locally re-registered in the country of Malta to KCY 919. Seen in the ownership of KopTaCo Coaches Co-op Ltd of Gzira in September 2011 at Qawra, 801 was new to Dix as a Ford R1114 and in Malta was fitted with an AEC engine. (Owen Woodliffe)

Former 810 (EYH 810V), seen here with Southwark Children's Foundation, was a regular visitor to the Victoria area of London during the early 1990s. (Brian Botley)

Former 170, previously 870 (B870 XYR), is seen here with Brown of Barway, Cambridgeshire (t/a A&D Coaches), in their yard during October 2009. They also owned 164 at the time. Both were acquired for school work in May 2005 from Thorpe's of Wembley, who had acquired them in March 2003. (Owen Woodliffe)

873 (B873 YYX) was the only Leyland Duple Caribbean II that was purchased. It was new in June 1985 and only lasted a few months in the fleet. It is seen here with Boardabus at the North Weald Bus Rally on 30 June 1996. (Andrew Mead)

'Here Comes the Sun', so 'Don't Pass Me By'; please buy your 'Ticket to Ride' before the 'Magical Mystery Tour' departs to take the 'Long and Winding Road' past the Cavern Club and through the 'Strawberry Fields Forever'! Former 874 (C874 CYX and now GEY 273), seen here with Maghull Coaches Ltd of Bootle, waits near Albert Dock in Liverpool before departing on a Beatles Magical Mystery Tour of Liverpool. (Owen Woodliffe)

Former Kent-based 877 (C877 CYX) was later acquired by Wilts & Dorset Bus Company subsidiary Hants & Dorset Motor Services (t/a Damory Coaches) and was numbered 5021 in their combined fleet. It waits at Swanage bus and railway station while on a local private hire on 17 July 2001. (Andrew Mead)

Former Dix FLA 998J, a Ford R226 /
Duple Viceroy, is seen here with Finchley
Coaches Ltd of Finchley, London, N12. It
enters the grounds of Ravenscroft School,
Totteridge, London N20, ready to operate
the after-school bus service between the
school and Totteridge & Whetstone station
on 15 June 1981. (The school was renamed
the Totteridge Academy in September 2011.)
(Andrew Mead)

Former 465 (EWF 465V) operated in Bath on the 'Citysightseeing' tour during May 2005 after
the batch passed to Ensign Bus, where it was converted for sightseeing work. It is seen here
outside Bath Abbey. (Andrew Mead)

814 (FYX 814W), now with Davian of Enfield, arrives at Wembley on 12 May 1990 for the FA Cup Final between south London club Crystal Palace and Manchester United, which ended in a 3-all draw. It had been acquired by Davian the previous month and retained its previous livery. (Phil Moth)

Former 814 (FYX 814W), now with County Bus, having been acquired from Davian, is seen in 'Sampson' livery in their yard in Gibbs Road, Edmonton, on 3 October 1993. (Andrew Mead)

925 (H925 XYT), together with a few of its sisters, was loaned to Independent Way (t/a Limebourne) for use on their LRT routes 42 and C10. Here is 925 on route C10, bound for Victoria station, in the Buckingham Palace Road contraflow bus lane outside Victoria coach station on 26 November 1998. The bus lane was removed during 2001 when the road became two-way once again. (Andrew Mead)

now XMD 47A). Another very well-known bus in preservation is double-deck, Alexander-bodied Volvo D10M 115 (F115 PHM). Arriva London restored 115 into almost original condition with assistance from Grey-Green's former chief engineer Ron Barnard. It has recently been donated to the London Transport Museum and can be viewed at their Acton depot site. Sister bus 143 (F143 PHM), now in private ownership, has also been restored to near original condition. It is kept at Yeldham Transport Museum, along with semi-preserved Leyland Lynx 801 (D101 NDW) and Leyland Leopard 817 (FYX 817W), both of which are in separate private ownership. Privately owned Leyland Lynx 887 (E887 KYW) is preserved in Maidstone & District livery.

In December 2010 former Grey-Green employee John Wilks registered a new company named 'Grey-Green Coaches Ltd' to protect the name. (Arriva still retain the company 'Grey-Green Ltd'.) The company is currently dormant. However, John acquired a Plaxton Paramount 3500 bodied Leyland Tiger coach, which at one time operated for Leaside Travel. It has been painted into Grey-Green flag livery. He has since sold the vehicle.

Bibliography

Books:

Bateman, K., *Operations of the George Ewer Group* (Ewer Group Enthusiasts' Club, 1978).

Bateman, K., *Services of the George Ewer Group* (Ewer Group Enthusiasts' Club, 1978).

Bateman, K., *World Wide Coaches Ltd – Fleet History* (Ewer Group Enthusiasts' Club, 1976).

Bateman, K., and Woodliffe, O., *60 Years of Coaching: The George Ewer Group 1919–1979* (Ewer Group Enthusiasts' Club, 1980).

Bateman, K., and Woodliffe, O., *The Grey-Green Story* (Capital Transport, 1986).

Bateman, K., and Woodliffe, O., *The Rise and Fall of British Coachways* (Rochester Press, 1984).

McLachlan, T., *Grey-Green and Contemporaries* (Arthur Southern, 2007).

Wilks, J., *Pride and Passion: My Life with Grey-Green Coaches* (Lulu, January 2012).

Woodliffe, O., *Grey-Green: From Ewer to Arriva* (Owen Woodliffe, 2001).

Other Publications:

Ewer Group Enthusiasts' Club and Grey-Green Enthusiasts' Club (newsletters 1966–2000).